I0430019

A BUSINESS APPROACH TO LIME FARMING

Complete Entrepreneurial Step By Step Guide To Lime Garden From Scratch

ZHURI HART

DISCLAIMER

This book is intended to provide general information and insights on adopting a business approach to farming. The content within is based on the author's knowledge and experiences up to the date of publication. It is essential to recognize that the field of agriculture is dynamic, influenced by various factors such as market conditions, climate, and regulatory changes.

Readers are advised to conduct thorough research, seek professional advice, and consider their unique circumstances before implementing any strategies or practices discussed in this book. The author and publisher disclaim any responsibility for the accuracy, completeness, or suitability of the information provided. The book is not a substitute for professional advice, and the author and publisher shall not be liable for any damages or losses arising from the use or reliance on the information presented herein.

Individual results may vary, and success in farming enterprises is contingent upon numerous variables. The author encourages readers to consult with relevant experts, agricultural extension services, and legal or financial professionals to tailor strategies to their specific needs and local conditions.

This book is not intended to be a comprehensive guide to all aspects of farming, and readers should exercise their judgment and discretion in applying the principles discussed. The author and publisher do not endorse any specific products, services, or companies mentioned in this book unless explicitly stated.

By reading this book, the reader acknowledges and accepts the inherent uncertainties in agricultural endeavors and agrees to use the information at their own risk.

TABLE OF CONTENTS

ABOUT THE BOOK

The invaluable manual "A Business Approach to Lime Farming" carefully examines the nuances of lime production with an emphasis on business tactics. This book is significant because it covers a wide range of important subjects, from advanced business and marketing tactics to the basic principles of lime farming. For new and seasoned lime farmers alike, this book is an indispensable tool that gives them the know-how to turn lime farming into a lucrative endeavor.

Setting the scene, the introduction provides a summary of lime farming while highlighting its critical function in agriculture. The significance of lime in agriculture is discussed, emphasizing both its ecological and economic value. The book's goals are spelled out, giving readers a road map for navigating the abundance of material that is offered.

The majority of the book explores important topics including knowing about different types of lime, getting the soil ready, and planting methods.

The thorough examination of crop management methods, such as fertilizer management, pruning procedures, and irrigation plans, equips farmers with the knowledge and skills necessary for productive lime farming. In addition, the thorough discussion of post-harvest management, harvesting, and disease and pest control gives readers the knowledge they need to minimize risks and maximize yields.

The book's emphasis on the commercial side of lime farming is one of its standout qualities. Understanding market demand, locating target markets, and creating successful marketing plans are all made easier with the help of the chapters on market analysis and marketing strategies. Offering readers advice on cost estimation, revenue projections, profitability analysis, and responsible financial management, financial planning is a major area of concentration.

With the use of case studies, which offer insights from profitable lime farms, the book gains a more practical aspect that helps readers modify tactics to fit their circumstances. With its examination of organic and sustainable lime farming and its talks about new technology and trends, this book presents itself as a forward-thinking manual for anyone hoping to succeed in the rapidly changing lime industry.

"A Business Approach to Lime Farming" is an extensive and innovative resource that goes beyond conventional agricultural manuals. Its focus on the business side, along with its useful advice and real-world examples, make it an indispensable resource for anyone looking to succeed and last in the lime farming sector.

CHAPTER ONE

LIME FARMING INTRODUCTION

Lime farming, sometimes referred to as citrus farming, is the practice of growing a variety of citrus fruits, among which lime is a notable member. Limes are little, green, citrus-derived fruits with a high acid content. Due to their unique flavor, they are commonly grown for both home and commercial use, and they are a common addition to food and drink recipes.

To highlight the importance of lime farming in agriculture, this introduction will examine the main facets of lime farming.

AN OVERVIEW OF LIME PRODUCTION

Cultivating lime trees, mainly those of the Citrus aurantiifolia and Citrus latifolia species, is known as lime farming. These evergreen trees need well-drained soil and enough sunlight to grow to their full potential; they do best in subtropical and tropical areas.

The careful planting of lime seeds or saplings follows the selection of appropriate planting locations as the first step in the cultivation process.

To maintain a robust and fruitful lime orchard, farmers need to be mindful of several aspects, including soil composition, irrigation, and insect management.

Lime trees are distinguished by their glossy green leaves and relatively tiny stature, with an average height of 6 to 13 feet. Lime trees yield oblong to rounded fruits with a smooth, thin peel that turns green or yellow when ripe.

A labor-intensive operation, lime farming necessitates close attention to disease control, fertilizing, and pruning at every stage of the growth cycle. The best time to harvest depends on the type of lime and the environment in the area. Generally, harvesting occurs when the limes reach the appropriate size, color, and acidity.

LIME'S SIGNIFICANCE IN AGRICULTURE

Lime is an important agricultural ingredient that has many uses outside of cooking. It is a precious commodity. Lime is an essential component of agricultural soil since it improves soil quality and stimulates plant development.

Acidic soils are treated with agricultural lime, which is typically applied as calcium carbonate, to balance their pH levels. This technique, called liming, improves nutrient availability and lowers soil acidity, which benefits crops by fostering a more conducive environment.

Lime is also a great source of vitamin C, which is an important component of human health. Its inclusion in the diet offers several advantages, including antioxidant qualities, skin health, and immune system support. Thus, lime cultivation helps to meet the nutritional demands of customers worldwide in addition to serving the agricultural sector.

The field of lime farming involves a labor-intensive growing procedure that aims to yield a product that is valuable for agriculture and cooking. Lime farming is a flexible and important part of the agricultural landscape, ranging from the meticulous maintenance of lime orchards to the wider impact on soil quality and human nutrition.

CHAPTER TWO

RECOGNIZING DIFFERENT TYPES OF LIME

COMMON TYPES OF LIME

Citrus fruits are popular because of their zesty flavor and range of culinary uses. Of all the citrus fruits, limes are my personal favorite because of their unique, tangy flavor that complements so many different foods. There are numerous types of limes, and each has special qualities, tastes, and uses.

FEATURES AND APPLICATIONS FOR EVERY VARIETAL

The Persian lime, sometimes known as Tahiti lime, is one of the most well-known types of lime. It is distinguished by its size, vivid green hue, and lack of seeds. Persian limes are a mainstay in the culinary arts, especially in mixed drinks and key lime pies. It is a well-liked option for both sweet and savory recipes because of its somewhat sweet and tangy flavor.

The Key lime, on the other hand, is smaller and has a unique yellow color when ripe. It is often referred to as the Mexican lime or West Indian lime. With its powerful scent and high acidity, the Key lime is rather powerful even in small form. This lime kind adds a strong, zesty zing to marinades, sauces, and cocktails. It is also frequently used in the well-known Key lime pie.

The Kaffir lime is another distinctive species of lime, distinguished by its distinct wrinkles and bumps on its skin. The fragrant leaves and zest of the Kaffir lime, which are native to Southeast Asia, are highly prized in Thai and Indonesian cooking. In particular, the leaves are often used to give soups, curries, and stir-fries a fragrant, lemony flavor.

HOW TO CHOOSE THE BEST VARIETY FOR YOUR FARM

Selecting the right lime variety for your farm requires taking into account several variables, such as the intended use in cooking, the climate, and the state of the land. Persian limes, for example, grow well in subtropical regions and are suitable for commercial cultivation on a wider scale. They are perfect for a variety of culinary applications due to their adaptable flavor and seedless nature.

Key limes do better in tropical areas due to their increased resistance to heat and humidity. Grown on a lesser scale or as a specialty, Key limes may be a satisfying option for you. Chefs and home cooks alike love Key limes for their unusual flavor profile, which provides a unique touch to desserts, drinks, and savory foods.

The Kaffir lime might be an intriguing addition to the farm for individuals looking into unusual and exotic possibilities. But for it to flourish, it needs a warm, tropical climate. Kaffir limes are in demand for their aromatic leaves and zest, therefore farmers who want to supply local markets or specialized culinary enterprises could find a market by growing them.

Knowing the common kinds of lime, their traits, and the best applications for them is essential to making wise choices while growing lime. Whether you choose the aromatic Kaffir lime, the spicy Key lime, or the widely known Persian lime, each type has unique traits of its own. You can start a profitable lime-growing business that meets the needs of both agriculture and cooking by matching your selection to the unique circumstances of your farm and the tastes of your intended audience.

CHAPTER THREE

GETTING READY FOR SOIL AND PLANTING

LIME TREE SOIL REQUIREMENTS

Like many other citrus species, lime trees do best on well-draining soils that range in pH from slightly acidic to neutral. For lime trees, the optimal pH range is normally 6.0 to 7.5. Because lime trees are sensitive to extremes in acidity or alkalinity, it is imperative to determine the pH level of the soil before planting. Lime plants suffer from root rot, which is brought on by poorly draining soils. Rich soils with lots of organic matter are preferred by lime trees in addition to pH and drainage. Compost or well-rotted manure can be added to the soil to improve its fertility and supply vital nutrients for the growth and development of trees.

GETTING THE SOIL READY FOR PLANTS

One of the most important steps in making sure lime trees are successfully established is proper soil preparation. First things first, remove any undesired plants, weeds, or rubbish from the planting area. This facilitates the establishment of a hygienic and favorable environment for the young lime trees. After clearing the area, test the soil to find out how fertile it is and what pH it contains. To attain the required pH range and nutritional balance, amend the soil according to the findings. When preparing soil, adding organic matter— such as old manure or compost—improves soil structure and increases nutrient availability.

Lime trees benefit from friable, well-aerated soil in terms of soil structure. Compacted or heavy soils can hinder the growth of roots and water penetration, resulting in problems such as roots that are wet. Think about tilling or loosening the soil to a minimum of 12 to 18 inches to solve this. As a result, the young lime plants can develop a robust and extensive root system and improve root penetration. To give the soil amendments time to fully integrate and stabilize before adding the lime trees, it is imperative to prepare the soil well in advance of planting.

THE BEST WAYS TO PLANT LIME TREES

A set of procedures must be followed while planting lime trees to maximize their chances of success. First, dig a hole deep enough and wide enough to easily fit the root ball of the tree. Take the tree out of its container slowly, taking care not to damage the roots too much. As you position the tree in the middle of the hole, make sure that the top of the root ball is just barely visible above the ground. To remove any air pockets, carefully compact the adjusted dirt as you backfill the hole.

To help the soil surrounding the roots of the recently planted lime tree settle, give it lots of water. Mulch is applied around the tree's base to assist retain moisture, prevent weed growth, and control soil temperature. During the early phases of establishment, proper watering is essential, but it's also critical to prevent soggy conditions. Lime trees require regular soil moisture monitoring and irrigation adjustments based on their needs.

A balanced fertilizer applied during the growing season also supplies the nutrients required for strong foliage, blooms, and fruit development.

Growing lime plants successfully depends on knowing and fulfilling the unique soil needs of these citrus trees. The finest conditions for lime trees to grow and produce an abundance of fruit can be created by meticulously preparing the soil and following planting guidelines.

CHAPTER FOUR

TECHNIQUES FOR CROP MANAGEMENT

TECHNIQUES FOR IRRIGATION AND WATERING

Using efficient irrigation and watering techniques is essential to crop management success. The idea is to minimize water waste while giving crops the right amount of water to promote their growth and development. One method that is frequently used is drip irrigation, in which a system of tubes and emitters delivers water straight to the base of plants.

This technique guarantees exact control over the amount of water each plant receives while simultaneously conserving water by lowering evaporation.

Timing is another crucial component of watering. Watering crops at the appropriate time of day is crucial to maximizing productivity and minimizing stress on the plants. Watering in the early morning or late at night helps reduce evaporation loss and enables plants to take up moisture when they are most responsive. Keeping an eye on soil moisture levels is also essential for tailoring irrigation schedules to the individual requirements of the crops.

LIME TREE TRAINING AND PRUNING

Lime tree training and pruning are essential orchard management techniques that improve fruit quality, tree health, and overall productivity. The process of pruning entails removing certain branches, shoots, or leaves to promote air circulation, manage size, and shape the tree. Pruning regularly lowers the chance of pest infestations, removes damaged or dead wood, and encourages the growth of robust, fruitful branches.

Lime trees can be trained to grow in a specific shape or structure by following certain guidelines. Techniques like trellising and staking can be used to accomplish this. When a tree is trained properly, sunlight reaches every area of the tree, which promotes photosynthesis and fruit development. It also makes pest control and harvesting simpler. Early training helps develop a robust and balanced framework for future growth, especially in young lime plants.

MANAGEMENT OF NUTRIENTS AND FERTILIZATION

A crucial component of crop management is fertilization, which is the process of adding necessary nutrients to the soil to promote the growth and development of plants. It is essential to comprehend the distinct nutrient needs of crops to attain maximum yields. Farmers can adjust their fertilization tactics to the specific crop's requirements by using soil testing, which is frequently used to evaluate the levels of nutrients in the soil.

The three main macronutrients—nitrogen, phosphorus, and potassium—are essential to plant nutrition. In smaller amounts, micronutrients including iron, zinc, and manganese are also vital. There are several ways to apply fertilizers, such as side-dressing, broadcasting, and fertigation (application by irrigation). Crop rotation, cover crops, and organic fertilizer use are examples of sustainable agricultural techniques that assist preserve soil fertility over time while reducing their negative effects on the environment.

Good crop management practices are critical to improving agricultural productivity while fostering sustainability and environmental stewardship. These practices include appropriate watering and irrigation, lime tree pruning and training, and strategic fertilization.

CHAPTER FIVE

CONTROL OF DISEASES AND PESTS

TYPICAL PESTS OF LIME TREES

Like any other crop, lime trees are vulnerable to a variety of pests that can harm them and reduce their productivity. The citrus psyllid (Diaphorina citri), which is well-known for spreading the bacteria that causes citrus greening disease, is one of the frequent pests that harm lime trees. These microscopic insects cause nutrient deficits and stunted growth by feeding on the sap of lime plants. The citrus leaf miner (Phyllocnistis citronella) is another major pest. The larvae of this pest burrow through the leaves, producing serpentine mines that hinder the photosynthetic capacity of the tree.

The brown soft scale and the cottony cushion scale are two types of scale insects that can harm lime trees by feeding on the sap of the plant. This feeding weakens the tree and can cause the honeydew that the scales expel to develop sooty mold. Other pests that can infest lime trees include aphids and mites, which can cause leaf deformation and spread viruses. It takes careful observation and prompt action to manage these pests and shield lime orchards from serious harm.

PATHOLOGIES IMPACTING LIME PRODUCTION

Numerous illnesses can affect the quality and amount of the harvest produced by lime farming. The bacterium Xanthomonas axonopodis is the cause of the contagious illness known as citrus canker, which affects lime trees. It appears as lesions on stems, leaves, and fruit, which causes defoliation and lower-quality fruit. The fungus Colletotrichum is the source of another prevalent disease called anthracnose, which can cause dark, sunken lesions on fruits and foliage and ultimately reduce the crop's marketability.

A viral disease known as citrus tristeza virus (CTV) can severely damage lime orchards by lowering tree health and productivity.

Phytophthora spp. is the culprit behind foot rot, a soil-borne disease that damages the tree's root system and causes it to wilt and eventually die.

An efficient disease management approach in lime farming must include the use of disease-resistant lime tree cultivars as well as good sanitation procedures, such as the removal and destruction of sick plant material.

STRATEGIES FOR INTEGRATED PEST MANAGEMENT (IPM)

The goal of integrated pest management (IPM), a comprehensive strategy for disease and pest control, is to reduce the need for chemical pesticides while encouraging ecologically safe and sustainable methods. Using IPM strategies in lime farming entails combining chemical, biological, and cultural control techniques. Cultural techniques, which lower the danger of pest and disease outbreaks and improve the general health of the orchard, include appropriate tree spacing and sufficient watering.

Biological management techniques entail the introduction of beneficial bacteria or predatory insects—natural enemies of pests. For example, releasing citrus psyllid-targeting parasitoid wasps can aid in population control. Furthermore, enhancing the ecosystem's natural equilibrium can be achieved by growing cover crops that draw beneficial insects. When necessary, chemical control methods are used, such as the sparing application of fungicides and insecticides, with an emphasis on choosing products that have the least negative effects on the environment and non-target organisms.

A key component of integrated pest management (IPM) is routine orchard monitoring to identify early indicators of disease or pest infestation. Farmers may efficiently manage pests and diseases while preserving the long-term viability of their crops by combining several tactics and customizing them to the unique conditions of the lime orchard.

CHAPTER SIX

HARVESTING AND MANAGING AFTER HARVEST

HOW TO CHOOSE THE APPROPRIATE TIME TO GATHER LEMONS

One of the most important factors that directly affect the fruit's quality and flavor is when to harvest limes. Lime maturity is usually assessed by combining characteristics like size, firmness, and color. When limes attain a desired color—typically a vivid green or yellow, depending on the lime variety—they are generally ready to be harvested. Another telltale sign is size; fully grown limes have a specified diameter that is safe to eat. To make sure the fruit is neither too soft nor too hard, its firmness is also evaluated.

METHODS OF HARVESTING TO GET THE HIGHEST YIELD

Using effective harvesting methods is essential to increasing the output of lime crops. One popular technique is hand harvesting, in which knowledgeable workers delicately remove the fruit from the trees. To protect the fruit and the tree, sharp pruning shears or harvesting knives are a must. There is also the option of mechanical harvesting, particularly in large-scale lime orchards. To prevent bruises or damage to the limes during harvesting, this approach needs to be calibrated carefully. By focusing on fully ripened fruits, selective harvesting guarantees a larger total yield while preserving the harvest's quality.

AFTER-HARVEST MANAGEMENT AND PRESERVATION

Lime shelf life and market value are strongly impacted by post-harvest management, which is an essential stage. The gathered fruit must first be thoroughly cleaned and sorted to get rid of any dirt or debris. The limes should next be meticulously assessed according to size, color, and quality. When it comes to keeping the fruit fresh throughout storage and transportation, packaging is crucial.

To minimize damage and allow for sufficient air circulation, sturdy, well-ventilated containers or boxes are frequently utilized.

Lime shelf life is greatly influenced by storage conditions. Controlled humidity levels in cold storage facilities aid in delaying the ripening process and preserving the fruit's freshness. Lime storage should never take place with other fruits that give out ethylene gas, since this can hasten ripening and shorten the lime's shelf life. It is crucial to keep an eye on the temperature and humidity levels during storage to stop the growth of mold and preserve the overall quality of the collected limes.

Precise scheduling, efficient harvesting methods, and careful handling and storage procedures are all necessary for successful lime harvesting and post-harvest management. Growers can maximize productivity and profitability by closely monitoring each of these factors to make sure their limes reach consumers in prime condition.

CHAPTER SEVEN

EVALUATING THE LIMES MARKET DEMAND THROUGH MARKET

ANALYSIS AND MARKETING STRATEGIES

A key component of creating a winning marketing plan is comprehending and evaluating the lime market's needs. The demand for limes is influenced by several factors, including consumer preferences, nutritional trends, and cultural influences. To estimate present demand and forecast future trends, market research is essential. Businesses can predict changes in lime demand by examining seasonal variations, purchasing trends, and consumption patterns.

In addition, researching rivals and their market share offers important perspectives on the dynamics of lime consumption. By doing a thorough analysis of the target demographic's preferences, including age groups, geographic locations, and income levels, firms can adjust their marketing strategies and product offerings appropriately. Furthermore, knowing how limes are used in various cuisines and culinary customs can point to interesting business sectors to investigate.

FINDING THE RIGHT TARGET MARKETS

An effective marketing strategy must identify the appropriate target markets. Behavioral patterns, psychographics, and demographics are thoroughly analyzed to help identify the target market categories that lime goods are most likely to appeal to. This entails being aware of the target audience's requirements, tastes, and spending power. For instance, although foodies may be more interested in limes' flavor-enhancing qualities, health-conscious consumers may be more drawn to their nutritional advantages.

Market segmentation based on factors like income, gender, age, and lifestyle enables the development of customized marketing messages that appeal to particular target audiences. Geographic segmentation also accounts for cultural and regional preferences, which helps companies tailor their marketing approaches to a wide range of customers. The efficacy of promotional endeavors can be further enhanced by partnerships with influencers or organizations that are in line with the chosen target markets.

CREATING SUCCESSFUL MARKETING PLANS

Creating marketing tactics that work for limes requires a complex strategy that incorporates several factors. In a market where competition is fierce, creating a value proposition that emphasizes the special attributes of limes is essential to standing out. Reaching a larger audience and interacting with potential customers is facilitated by using a variety of marketing channels, such as social media, digital platforms, and traditional advertising.

Another essential element in the creation of a marketing plan is strategic pricing. Setting competitive and appealing rates requires examining the pricing methods of rivals, taking manufacturing expenses into account, and comprehending the market value of limes. Promoting products, offering discounts, or combining them can also increase demand and boost revenue.

Lime products must have strong brand recognition and a positive brand image to succeed over the long run. Brand loyalty is influenced by quality control, consumer involvement, and consistent message. Customer feedback can be gathered and used to inform continuing product and marketing strategy improvements. Lastly, ensuring that marketing tactics are flexible and responsive to market movements guarantees their long-term efficacy and relevance.

CHAPTER EIGHT

PLANNING YOUR FINANCES FOR LIME FARMING

CALCULATING THE EXPENSES OF GROWING LIME

Since cost estimation offers a thorough grasp of the financial requirements involved in the entire cultivation process, it is an essential component of financial planning for lime farming. This covers costs for clearing land, planting seedlings or saplings, irrigation systems, labor, equipment, fertilizers, and pesticides, among other overheads. Precise cost calculation facilitates the effective allocation of resources and enables farmers to make well-informed investment decisions in lime farming.

The expense of land preparation, which includes tasks like leveling, plowing, and soil testing, is a major factor. Another crucial element is choosing premium seedlings or saplings, as this has a direct impact on the productivity and general prosperity of the lime farm. Furthermore, it's important to carefully estimate ongoing costs for things like pesticides and fertilizers while taking the condition of the soil, the temperature, and the frequency of pests into account. The effectiveness of lime farming activities is enhanced by the implementation of contemporary irrigation methods and equipment, which is also a critical factor in cost estimation.

FORECASTS OF REVENUE AND ANALYSIS OF PROFITABILITY

Forecasting revenue from lime farming entails taking into account variables such as market demand, anticipated yield, and pricing patterns. To comprehend customer preferences, industry dynamics, and possible competitors, in-depth market research is crucial. Several variables, such as the kind of soil, the climate, and the farming methods used, might affect yield estimates.

Beyond revenue estimates, profitability analysis considers all of the expenses related to lime farming.

To calculate the net profit, deduct the predicted costs from the anticipated revenue. To ensure a true assessment of the financial sustainability of lime farming, farmers should take both fixed and variable expenses into account.

Financial viability in lime production requires constant observation and revision of predictions in response to market changes and unanticipated obstacles.

FINANCIAL MANAGEMENT AND BUDGETING ADVICE

A key component of good financial management in lime farming is creating an effective budget. Farmers should create a thorough budget that details all anticipated costs and allots funds appropriately. This involves setting aside money for labor, equipment upkeep, irrigation systems, fertilizer, insecticides, seedlings, land preparation, and any future crises.

A well-organized budget acts as a guide, assisting farmers in staying within their means and making wise choices.

Risk reduction techniques and income source diversification are further financial management advice for lime farmers. Investigating different revenue streams, such as selling goods made of limes or taking part in regional markets, can be an element of diversification. Insurance coverage for unanticipated events like bad weather, insect outbreaks, or market swings is one type of risk reduction strategy.

Keeping abreast of technical developments and implementing cost-effective farming techniques can also boost output and cut expenses, improving financial results. Lime farming businesses need to regularly assess and modify their financial plans to adapt to shifting market conditions and unforeseen obstacles.

CHAPTER NINE

PRINCIPLES OF SUSTAINABLE AGRICULTURE:

SUSTAINABLE AND ORGANIC LIME FARMING

Sustainable lime farming is built on a set of principles that prioritize environmental health, social responsibility, and economic viability. One key principle involves soil health management, emphasizing the use of organic matter and cover crops to enhance soil fertility, structure, and water retention. Crop rotation is another vital aspect, preventing the depletion of specific nutrients and minimizing the risk of pest and disease outbreaks.

Water conservation is integral to sustainable lime farming, emphasizing efficient irrigation practices and water recycling.

The goal is to reduce water usage and prevent pollution of water resources. Biodiversity preservation is also central, promoting the cultivation of diverse crops and the preservation of natural habitats to support beneficial organisms and ecosystems.

Furthermore, sustainable lime farming emphasizes minimal use of external inputs such as synthetic fertilizers and pesticides, opting instead for natural alternatives and integrated pest management strategies. This approach reduces the environmental impact and supports long-term agricultural resilience.

ORGANIC PRACTICES FOR LIME FARMING

Organic lime farming follows strict guidelines to ensure the production of high-quality, chemical-free fruit. Soil health takes precedence, with the use of organic fertilizers like compost and manure. Cover cropping and intercropping play a crucial role in maintaining soil fertility and preventing erosion.

Weed management in organic lime farming relies on mulching, hand weeding, and the use of natural herbicides, avoiding the use of synthetic chemicals. Pest control involves the integration of natural predators, crop rotation, and the application of organic insecticides if necessary. These practices contribute to the overall health of the ecosystem and promote a balanced and sustainable farming system.

CERTIFICATION AND MARKET OPPORTUNITIES

Obtaining organic certification is a significant step for lime farmers looking to tap into the growing market for organic produce. Certification ensures that the farming practices comply with established organic standards, instilling confidence in consumers about the environmental and health benefits of the product. Certification may be provided by various organizations and adherence to these standards can open doors to premium markets.

The market for organic limes has witnessed substantial growth as consumers increasingly prioritize health and sustainability. Organic lime farmers can access premium prices and niche markets by meeting the demand for chemical-free, environmentally friendly produce. Additionally, consumers are often willing to pay a premium for certified organic products, creating a valuable market opportunity for lime farmers who embrace sustainable and organic practices.

Sustainable and organic lime farming is rooted in principles that prioritize environmental stewardship, biodiversity, and resource efficiency. Implementing organic practices not only ensures the production of high-quality, chemical-free limes but also opens up lucrative market opportunities through organic certification. As consumers become more conscious of the environmental and health impacts of their choices, the demand for sustainably produced organic limes is likely to continue its upward trajectory.

CHAPTER TEN

FUTURE TRENDS IN LIME FARMING

EMERGING TECHNOLOGIES IN AGRICULTURE

The future of lime farming is inevitably intertwined with the rapid advancement of emerging technologies in agriculture. Precision farming, powered by technologies such as GPS, sensors, and drones, is transforming the way lime orchards are managed. These tools enable farmers to monitor and optimize various factors, including soil health, water usage, and pest management.

The integration of data-driven insights and automation is enhancing efficiency, reducing resource wastage, and ultimately improving overall yields in lime farming.

Additionally, the utilization of artificial intelligence (AI) and machine learning (ML) is becoming more prevalent, providing farmers with predictive analytics for better decision-making in crop management.

INNOVATION IN LIME FARMING PRACTICES

Innovative farming practices are reshaping the landscape of lime cultivation, aiming for sustainability, increased productivity, and reduced environmental impact. One notable trend is the adoption of vertical farming techniques, allowing farmers to maximize space utilization and cultivate limes in controlled indoor environments. Hydroponics and aeroponics, which involve growing plants without soil, are gaining popularity, offering efficient nutrient delivery systems and minimizing water usage. Furthermore, advancements in breeding techniques, such as genetic modification and CRISPR technology, are contributing to the development of lime varieties with enhanced disease resistance, improved yield, and better adaptability to varying environmental conditions.

ADAPTING TO CLIMATE CHANGE

As climate change continues to pose challenges to agriculture, lime farmers are actively seeking strategies to adapt and mitigate its impact. Variability in temperature, water scarcity, and extreme weather events necessitate resilient farming practices. Diversification of lime varieties and the introduction of heat-tolerant and drought-resistant strains are becoming crucial adaptation measures. Water management is also a key focus, with the implementation of efficient irrigation systems and rainwater harvesting to ensure optimal hydration for lime orchards. Additionally, the integration of agroforestry practices, such as planting cover crops and incorporating natural vegetation, aids in soil conservation and climate resilience by reducing erosion and enhancing biodiversity.

The future of lime farming is marked by a synergy of emerging technologies, innovative practices, and adaptive strategies in response to the challenges posed by climate change.

www.ingramcontent.com/pod-product-compliance
Lightning Source LLC
Chambersburg PA
CBHW070828290526
45795CB00002B/878